ZIRCONIA

FENCEbooks

Published in the United States by

Fence Books
14 Fifth Avenue, #1A
New York, NY 10011
212-254-3660
www.fencebooks.com

Cover art by   Scott Dolan

Book design by   Saturnalia Books

Printed in Canada by   Westcan Printing Group

Fence Books is distributed by   University Press of New England
www.upne.com

Library of Congress Cataloging in Publication Data
        Minnis, Chelsey
        Zirconia / Chelsey Minnis [1970–]
        "Winner of the 2001 Alberta Prize"

Library of Congress Control Number: 2001093168

ISBN 0-9663324-8-2

First Edition

The author would like to acknowledge the editors of the following magazines, in which some of these poems have appeared: *Antonym, Chicago Review, Cream City Review, Faucheuse, Fence, Kenning, Provincetown Arts, Rain City Review,* and *The Seneca Review.* Grateful acknowledgement is also made to the Alberta duPont Bonsal Foundation, to Tom Thompson, and to the editors of Fence Books. Serious thanks to Robert Minnis, Doris Hellinghausen, Michelle Minnis and Peter Mayerson. Also to Brian Christopher Hamilton, Ruth Tobias, Joshua Clover, and Jeff Clark.

for Edward Dorn

TABLE OF CONTENTS

A SPEECH ABOUT THE MOON

I think, "The moon is mine and all the craters are mine."

Then I begin to think, "I am covered with drizzling grief.", "I have all the ice blue sinning birds.", "I control the sea.", and "Everything sticks out of the sea."

Then I plunge my hand into the air and say, "I want to eat the fighting swordfish in the sea who stick their swords in boats!" And, "I want to eat their swords."

Plus, "I like sultry avenging birds.", "Terrible birds with moisturized wings over the sea." and "I want to fight."

Then I think about the hazel waves of the ocean and the hot creamy lemon grasses of the moon.

I think, "I am going to sleep" and "I am dreaming about grey hair." and I lie very still for awhile. I think, "I can strew daisies in grey hair..."

Then I start to cry and the tears flow down to my teeth. I think, "Everyone has to bite silver mesh."

I constantly try to think, "Fish are resting in the sea." or "Some fish are just hanging in the sea."

And I lie very still and tell myself, "...In the middle of the night...it is totally quiet...no crabs are coming towards you..."

Then I sit up and cup my hands over my nose and shake my head slowly back and forth.

The world rises up on both sides of me. I think, "I have to die."

Then I lie in a position for awhile.

The moon is flapping and curling around me.

I think clearly, "I have to lie facedown." or else "The moonlight is smoothed on my back like the map of someone who is trying to leave."

Then I reluctantly think, "Dominating bluebirds.", "…that fly…", "around" and "…melon raptors…" and "Tricolor murder hawks.", "…with their songs."

I lie on my side so that the tears from one eye slide into the other eye.

I say, "I have to invent warm tawny roses that have never been seen before…"

Then I fix the sheets which are twisted around my ankles and think, "I have to be tormented."

Then I continue to think things about the moon, like, "The moon is a silver hitching ball…shorn…off the trucks of the world…."

I tell myself, "…late at night…a placid sea monster…is rising out of the sea…with kelp on its head…to look at me…"

I think about the moon again. "The moon is a silver leg-iron.", "My entrails are the color of moonlight."

Then I think about the circulating birds.

I rub my hands on my stomach and think "oh no" and start to cry.

I pull the long tears out of my eyes and look away.

Slow blinks crash down.

Then I hold my wrist very tightly and watch the veins rise up so I become vascular in the moonlight.

I think, "Birds are automatically beautiful" and twist around.

I am dragging the satin around in my mind and thinking of my displeasure. I roll over.

I cry more tears that spread across my face and think, "No, no, no", "Fish are biting the ocean."

I think, "The thoughts are like terrible ballet teachers with canes."

BIG DOVES

....
....
....
....doves
are rolling out of my heart...and...
............just rolling out of my heart..
....
....
....
....and molten ice is twisting out of my
heart like a frozen.......drink...because
............doves are flapping..in my..............................
.......heart...
....
and hustling around...and streaming..long.............
banners of wrath..
....
....
....

....

because...

....what is terrible!................................

................is diaphanous...........................and whatever.......................................

...........else I want to be..............................slaked..flashed......hauled...............turned

into a block of salt....................................placed in front of an..............elk and licked

into...........................different shapes...

....

....................or attacked............and thrown into the.............sea............................

...............................and tousled...

....and flung..................

....so that the wrath spills out of my heart.............

in curls..

....

....

....and I am......................................

..............................lowered...

....onto..................

....sand.

....

....because.............

I have come with the comfortable doves..

..................to accomplish...

.........my soft ideas...and..

....

................the doves are shy..

....rollers......

....who roll around and feel very suede or matte and......

beige with diaphanous talons...

..............and are very succulent and available in the body.....................................

.........because they flap around......................in the areas................................

of the heart...

....

....that I want....

to be..............flexed..........thrashed.................................spiraled and....................

neurally lathed..

....

....

....

....doves...

come as I wish...
....
....to emit a pang...............of........
softness.........................and.......to load a........................caress.............................
....into my heart...................................which is reinforced
by wrath.........................and soaked with growls...
....
....sashed with ache......................
....
................and has...............................pearl...........inlays of doom........................
....that...............
.......warring...blended doves...
....
.........................must pull and pull out of the zones..
....
....
....
................and then rove......around...
....with an overall...............effect
....
....

....of.....................liquid drumrolls..............

....

.......................and soft grappling hooks.......that pry........hard gasps off my mouth.....

.like shells..

....

....

....

...........................doves..

....

....

....with modern....opaque sides.......................

...........hot round souls..

....and the ability to haul..................

...perfumed sedative material.....................out of my heart......................................

....

....

.............this is a moment...

....or an..

.........upward waterfall..

....................appearing........and revealing to me now...

....

....curved.....................................

..........galaxy...

.................roseate...

....

..........aplomb........hauteur.......epitome.....................slams....................................

....................lasers...deep emotions...............................

....

...............................awe...

....lucre..............................

....

.....................napes..

....

....

....vales...

....

....

....

....

....

..........lava...

....

....

....

....

....

....

....

....

..........and anything else...

....

PITCHER

....

....

......................you have to take a metal pitcher with a wooden handle and just pour...........

.............the translucent contents over your head..

....and gasp...................................

....

....as the sting flashes sheer...................................

............................and the water forms..............a square vinyl veil...........................

..........or millimeter thin waterfall..

....over you....................................

....for a split second....................................

....

.............and the fringe drips..

........................like spangles or paillettes sewn singly on the edge...........................

......and the pear phase...................of a drop.......................repels...........................

....and then smears..................

....

....the bouncy..........moisture...........................

.......................against you..

..........and the fabric of your shirt is transformed by the drops pressed into the weave..........

......................to deliver clear panes of your shoulders and chest..............................

....

................and there are ringlets of water upon you..

....

....................as you fling........the pitcher down onto the brick road..........................

....and stand there..

.......with a cat intensity in your eyes..

....and wet strips of hair....................

....

....................and....................although...

....

....the metal pitcher clangs.....on the road.and.......rolls........

....................and.rolls..and.rolls..................

....to indicate the passage of time.......................

..........the sensual moment keeps splashing and unbuckling upon you like a replay............

..............and the waters keep redescending........from an airlock............to reveal..........

....

................the spitting beauty of your face......

UH

..uh..........I want to wear hot pants...

....

....and rest my boot on the back

of a man's neck...

....

....and........

....take a sharp cane..........

.....................and................stick my heart...............................like...a piece of trash

...........in a park...

.................and..

....

....

rise out of arctic waters with curled icicles in my hair and a speargun................................

....

....and.......................................

.........buy a lazy game cat with claws........................that scratch me..........................

....and..............................uh!....................

....

....

....

....................someone should knock me down...and press me against blue tile...............

....and shuck....................

a gold sheath dress.....................off me...

....and push...........................

.......a shiny buzzer...

...................to make me slide down a glistening chute...

....

....because....................I am sique...............

....

....

.....................................of everyone and opposed to everyone....................and just want

....

....

....to pluck the grey beards of old men...

....

....and...

....give them....

...........hairline fractures...

...............and a row of forest green stitches...................above their right eyes...............

....

......or then just...

...............bleed in a sailor suit..........................and salute them and faint..................

....

....so.......................they can bang

my mouth against a balcony railing.......................................or..............................

....cut my head off...

....

...................................because I am too......................petulant..........................

....

....

....

....and.......................................I.......want them to..

....centre death blows between.........

....my shoulder blades...and..................then......

....gently lick electrodes.......and stick

them to my temples..

....

.......................because..

....

.............................I must...

....

....take a silken pull cord...............................

and pull......it..

...........................and fall through a trapdoor...............................and....................

...............escape on a chrome war sleigh drawn by arctic huskies................and............

....uh........................

................................someone should...............................come towards me............

...........frowning with a knife..

....

....and butterfly my flesh...

....

...............and...try to.....................................

...........................give me...

....oral...................maxillofacial kisses................

....

............and then hit me with a brickbat..

....

............and shoot me........with round plump bullets................while I'm lounging.........

...............with a leopard pillow...

.....................because.........................uh..

....

....otherwise...................................

.......tears slide out from under my cat-eye sunglasses.............

FUR

................I'm ready to plunge into furs...................and reject the standards of my past...

........which allowed no warm furs to enclose...

....me and no fur linings.......................

....or strips of fur..............................

....on bare skin..

....

....and I could not bury my face in anything soft

.......................as I used to correlate a bad conscience with the...................................

....repetitive circular hand caress of

...a soothing material.....such as fur................as I have seen it happen before...................

.........................when someone doesn't say anything for 7–9 seconds.........................

....and you observe the cycles..................................

........of their hand through the fur..

.......................or they.............wrap a fur strap around their fists...................until....

......the sphere of musing bursts................and they say.........nothing to you...................

....which indicates a conscience ensconced.......

..........in a faux solace and limned...

..........with a relief...

....a conscience consumed with an undisclosed serious concern...

.................installed in a plush locus...

....cannot forgive itself........and..

.....surrounds itself with a valence of ermine..

....that insists on being stroked with sincere denial..............

....

.................I still believe in the need for honor and the refusal of fur stoles....................

....but I forgive........................

.........the desire for an inhuman softness...

....

....as many people are furious with themselves.......

while wearing clothes of the highest quality...

.....................and they are both disgraceful and touchable......................................

.............................as they caress their sleeves.................and wrap themselves........

.................or embalm their bad conduct in belly fur......in the loveless fur void bereft........

....of anything except comfort..............

....

....

SHOCKWAVE

....struck by translucent lightning...............

....or........

........................kneeling in milk near frayed wire...

....an icing white force.................

...............bursts from your brow..

....splits and rustles.............

.................................and tumbles down your face.......................................

.........................and pours over..

....your right eye...

....and ripples down....................................

....

.....................................and...

..............shines like.........broken light-blue eggs...

....

........................and has.........................the very lightest glints............................

..........of scallions or pearls.............bouncing on marble floors........or.........................

.........the silver lips of a feverish child......................or a thousand feathers.................

....free-falling........................

......................in a room with no swans...

..............................or...

....

............it flows like............coconut milk or......a saline drip.......................................

...................down...

...................the beard of an old man......who..............drinks venom.........................

...from a vein...on your ankle..................

....because...........................

....a.......charmed snake............twined

...........around you...

..........................or...

....you wore............

..................silver scissors around your neck in the rain..................................or.........

...............were smashed with a vial of cream.............in the skull...............................

...........or a glass candy dish of semen.....

MAROON

....................my bloodsticky...................................wet......................................

....

....baby...................................

..........is..................an auburn...and.............bloody......beauty..............................

............who..

.......shined......inside.....................a slippery milky sac.......................................

....on the grass...

...........and then...

.......kicked and kneed the sac until.................it thinned in a spot and split open.............

....and spilled out...............................

.............my steamy...clenched...................................

......fine-boned..

....knock-kneed...

.....................................baby..

...............my shaky.............collapsible.................baby whose legs.........................

...........are creaky...

....and who is...

..........sleepy and strong..

..............with matted fur and saline.....................and stickiness.................

.........and is falling down...

...........................on the grass..

.............and is my cockeyed.................................lop-eared....................................

....dewy...............baby..............................

....

....and at sunset................

....I am still trying to tear and bite and strip away.................

.....the membrane and marine blood as my...

................................glistening rusty....................drunk baby blinks her eyes...........

....

.............at the beautiful sultry carny show in the distance......

SECTIONAL

.......I sink into a reverie in leather...........................sectional couches........................

...........with caramel in my mouth...

....so that I am reliving...

....a moment and revolving........................

...............caramel as I am surrounded on all sides by...

.......................soft panels of genuine...

....

...................leather.....and I run my hand along the leather unknowingly........................

....

...........as I oralize the caramel and soften it as I am...

....

....loosening and loosening...............

.....................into my dreaminess....with a far-off composure............................and...

....

................................launching my molars.............into the cluster...........................

in order to.....locate...

...........the nucleus..

...........................of the caramel with my mouth and...........maul the unformed mass....

........................with my tongue..

..........and really lounge...

.............in the passive leather..

.....sectional...couch...with 12 separable sections..alone...

....

....

....as I try to evaluate....................the reverie...............

..............in the enormous moments...

on the couch made of soft skins...that are compressed...

....

...............................as I chew the mutable caramels.....................................

....and clench.........

my jaw...and demolish them.................................

.................in the durable moments..

....

.....................with a soft formation in my mouth............and the memories..................

....that are unavoidable.........................

....

............and the pliable anger......towards myself...

..........for lazing on tender leather...

...................................and hauling up the............delicate past............................

....

....on the casual............................

....

.......modular couch with padded armrests...

....where I can rest my arms

....as I revisit sorrowful.....and frightening moments...of happiness that must have occurred...

CHERRY

....................................I see you are kneeling...

....

......on the bone-marrow red.......wood floor...........and you want to grind your sorrows....

....into it..............

....

.........and twine your sorrows into the grain..

....or just cry on the bloodflecked.............

......wine-soaked sunburned surfaces...

..........with the smashed and polished spirals of grain.....................and the knotholes.......

....

.........you are sprawled on the auburn woodgrain..............and the sunwarmed...............

..........dusty beaten wood floor...

...................with the scars of burns and the chairscrapes..

....

....you want to touch the warps and knots...

.........................of the beautiful hand-laid..

....thirsty...russet.....................wood.................

........and plunge into the whorl...

...........................where the grain encloses a flaw or swerves...................................

.....around it..

....the beautiful burgundy wood.......................................

..............fed on blood...

.....................................with the long-boned grains..

..........and the scar of dragged spurs....................or the soft scuff marks from the...........

....drunk waltzes...........................

..............the wood that resembles the swollen pond...........enclosing.........................

......the thrown stone.............or the stain of the..

....expanding pool...of rosebrown headwound blood.................

.....that.............absorbs and throbs through the grain...

...................or the stain of the........punchbowl slosh...............or grown branch..........

....

........I see you are kneeling.............and raunchily........or ironically........scrubbing.........

........the floors with your.........naughty manual labor................................but............

.....you want to whisper your fears into the ear swirls of the wood.....................

SUPERVERMILION

...........supervermilion..infrared...........
....warpath..
....
....bloodlines......
....
...............fireballs..
....
...........redwoods...
....
....
.....................heartshaped..
....
....
....
....
....burned.......
....
.... nothing
....
....
....

....

....

....

....

....

....

....

....

....

....

....

....

....

....

....

..............rosy flames flap out of vents...

..................................hot pink gills flare on the tropical fish...............................

....

....lathers.......roll up in your veins........and splash in your heart.....as....................you...

....inhale the....

....

....

....

....

....

....

....

......................supervermilion..

....

....

....transfusion...............

....

....

....

.....................lush..

..............uranium rays...

..................come out of your eyes...

....

....

....you wrap space..........................

around your wrist...........................and pull it in...

........as.........wrath curves around you..........like a fume of smoke curves...................

....around a cupid fountain spurting fire.................

....

....

....supervermilion.....................

....bursts..........................flecks......

....mesh...........

....

....

....rampage.......

...................................persimmon...

....

....[go right into **BABY VAMP**]

BABY VAMP

....brain fever...................................

....

....

....

....

....

....

....

....

....

....

............all the thermometers......split open and pour...

....

....

...............................they lift you............so your head lolls..

....

....and..

.............put you in the clawfoot tub with crushed..........ice...

....

...................and....................................open the skylight...

.......so the fresh night is...black............and quick............

....and the breezes shine.................

...................your cheeks..

....and a drop of moisture on the middle of your lower lip...................forms...................

....

...............as you burn on clean sheets...

and dream of sealskin...

....and..

....burned mincemeat.....................

....

....

.........you are in a dreamstate...

.......with...

...metallic sepia lipstick smeared on your mouth.........bee wings stuck to your cheeks...........

.............and.................soft..........frizzed hair..

....

....

....

....as you lift your face up......with hot trust.................

..................and a fresh black velvet ribbon around your neck...................................

....your mouth like a sugarplum...........................

....

.............with translucent honey-toned baby teeth.......

REPORT ON THE BABIES

A baby on 9/16 only wanted to lean over and chew the stroller bar. I have ridden before on the bus with many small infants, roundheads and chewers, but none so emphatic or singleminded with preference for the stroller bar.

I have seen four babies arranged perfectly equidistant around the table (9/29).

I emphasize that this was not the only incident of four babies arranged perfectly equidistant around a table in a public establishment or café. Also, more emphatically, I have begun to discern two babies on a diagonal.

This is becoming more and more emphatic as the diagonals multiply and the connectors start to crisscross the city and leave marks like a grilled lamb chop. Also the obscene connectors are invisible and stick together.

Let me insist that I have also seen a baby with a red birthmark and perfectly calm, a baby crying directly behind in a movie theatre with no consolation 10/21, on a bus to Pittsburgh a baby could not stop arching its back 8/21, baby with pink headband constricting 9/13, a baby throwing down the chew-toy three times in my favorite café, baby who emphatically did not want the bottle, but agreed to eat a chip (on diagonal) 10/24, numerous babies inside baby seats on top of tables in cafés all over the city, one baby seat completely covered with a blanket suspected to contain a baby 11/1, also baby with bow scotch-taped to the head and baby with pacifier hanging on ear 10/29, 11/29. Let me more emphatically suggest that many of these babies and more are arranged perfectly equidistant and diagonal across the city.

Recently, this situation has become even worse. I've seen the babies fall in love with me when their parents have no idea. A baby on 9/11 was definitely in love with me and the parents did not know. A series of babies stronger and stranger than any before has been peeking at me. They continue to peek at a critical rate. Moreover, they seem to be enthralled in a rapture.

This heightened peeking has resulted in stress for both me and my acquaintances. One acquaintance recently revealed that she could no longer have lunch with me in a café because of the peeking.

The babies peek strongly when I'm waiting for my favorite bus drivers. They threaten to startle the bus drivers on their routes and confuse the dispatcher. The babies continue to insist strongly and you can see through their red hair they are in love. They say, "I love you...Come hold me over your head so I can swim...My parents don't know...I want you to have this chip..." Because of this emphatic peeking I almost went and held a baby over my head. They say, "My parents won't stop you...Swimming in the high seas..."

My former boss's baby continues to peek much more strongly than usual and says, "I'm over here...My head is round...I want to go up..."

I have tried to discourage the singular peeking but they continue to look at me with their eyes. When I try to walk right past them, they extend their arms and diagonals flow across the city....

UNCUT

...I desire to be pushed or shoved down....in a grassy area..

....and this is a real hope.....................

....but it is not possible.............

....to be held in the uncut grasses....with confidence..........and patience..........................

...........as the soft patterns crush beneath you...

........and you struggle to...............understand your resistance....................................

....

....to the design of the grass engraved on.........

....the skin.....of your bare limbs as you are...................

....forced............to blend.................

.................the inhalation of the scent with the coercion...

...................into a prominant and unwanted imprint......................................which.

....

.......resurfaces....in the presence of the technical stimulus..................or else the nuance....

....

...............to reframe you in the scenic grasses where there will be no discussion.................

....

....as the...............

.......grass blades press into the underside..

....

.......as you are driven down with a knee between your legs...

.......and you are trusted and pushed down with hope...

....

and held..

....

....

....until you retain..........................

......an incredibly accurate neural concept of the occurrence....................................

....................which you thoroughly misunderstand..in that moment..........................

as..........the scent adheres............to your receptors....upon....................................

............................the intake of breath...

....

....................and instills the peripheral vision of viridescence.............................

....and an airborn internal knowledge................

...............lands like a meteor and burns an outline..

...................of silence in the rustle...

....and you sink into....................................

...........a moment like a solarium..

....

...............and realize the honor...........of the offensive generous impulse.....................

..as you never believed you would be shoved against a soft green background to be admired...

....

...........and then instantly released.........from the...

....format of grasses......................

....

...............to persist within the sunwarped dome.....of 2–35 seconds............................

...........until...

....................the timeline.........resumes...

...........the sonic gnats...........and the sizzling daylight...

....implants you with the conjoined dewy moments...........

....

...........................so that you always remember the unfinished permanent interlude........

....

................with the noisy grasses and the fractured octagons of................................

........sunlight and the slow.............................absorption of the bee-buzz.................

....

....

....

...................................as your memory is now like a ball gown with grass stains..........

...because of the impression wrought by the insistence of a person who would not let you go..

THE SKULL RING

I am very excited about the skull ring. I didn't know anyone would think I wanted a silver skull ring. Now, when I am rude to those who oppose me, I can just look down at the skull ring. It has ruby chips in the eyes! Ruby chips like the nasty flame in my own eyes when I am insulted or reviled. No one will dare oppose me now in my hometown. For a very long time I have avoided rings because none of them seemed right for me. A skull ring is actually a good complement to my diabolical will. Thank you very much for the skull ring.

PRIMROSE

............when my mother...

...........................was raped..

....

......a harpsichord began to play...

....red candles melted.....and..................

...........spilled down the mantle...

....there was blood in the courtyard...

.....................and blood on the birdbath...

....and blood drizzled....on brown flagstones...

...........................as a red fox bared its teeth...

.....................white harts.............froze...

......and snow-hares fled...and left.......

....heartshaped footprints in the snow..............................

....that melted............

....

.......in the spring when I was born..

....

....

....

.................and it is torture.......for my mother............................that I am now luscious

....and she is dead.

....

....

........and that I have...

.........................bare shoulders..

....and a flower behind my ear.....................

....

....

......as I beat gentleman rapists..

....

..............with bronze statuettes..

...........so that the blood...........................oozes down their handsome sideburns...........

....or give them.......................

.....a poisoned mushroom..

....

....or corsages and corsages of gunshot

TIGER

...........................spattered lilies............with their...............recurved..............

.............petals.........and suffusions..

....are breathless and....

.....dangerous...

....

.........................flowers..that you hold in your hands.............as you stride..............

.............through the garden...

....

.................................with your petulance.................................

........and your self-punishment..................and your extravagant disappointment..........

....

....

the hungriness..

of the bloomed..........................flowers with the thrust of the florets.......................

...............................that are 4–6 inches across......................................

....

.............as you go toward them...

.......................you see their outward development................................

.........as they are................like sprung traps.......................................

.....................................the flecked lilies...........that you carry around...............

.................make you feel...........tasteless and overjoyed...

....

........because they have no restraint...........as they are opened flowers.........................

............with no reserves.......although...

....they get deeper and deeper in their funnels..........

....

....

....

....

....

...........and have the appearance...........of a fine wine thrown...................................

.......against a wall..

....they seem to be marvelous...........

........as I think about...........................how I want to replicate...............................

..........them or re-create their arcs..

.............................or put them in a spotlight...

...............against a black backdrop..

....or lower them into.........

........a glass case........with a humidifier.........and a temperature control......................

...............and watch the needles...

44

....graph their life force...............

....

....

....they are......preserved objects...

..........in the controlled environments...

....under heat lamps......................

....

..........nurtured and nurtured.....to turn into the desired unruly organisms....................

....you can place...................................

....in a beautiful.....unbroken vase......................

....

....or...

....in refrigerated trucks.......................................

....

....as you like their..................................

....expansiveness.............

..............and the difficult angles...

....

..............and the compression..

....

....

………as they express a generous hunger.………so that you may……………………………

…………………………not fear……………………………………………………………………………………………

such a property within yourself or.……others……………………………………………………………………

……or………………………

…………………………demonstrate an unusual loud vulnerability that is forgivable……………

………and vulgar…………………………and causes you to.……progress in your understanding.……

………………of combinations of bad behaviors…………………………………………………………………

………

………

………

………

……………lilies with the yellow throats…………and floppy leaves………………………………

…………………that you have to leave alone……………………………………………………………………

………

……………………………………like show girls…………………………………………………………………………

………

………………………………………the soft apricot/orange coloration with brownish spark-burns.

………of the daylilies.………that live in the day………………………………………………………

………

…………………your emotion forms……………………………in response to their presence.………

…………and the fearsome hunger……………………………………………………………………………………

....resurged by the............................

....oblanceolate..

..............unpleasantly scented............................hairy blooms..............................

.................................whose bulbs...

...................................are..

...................dried.................................in the sun..

..................and eaten with reindeer milk in some parts of Russia.............

STERNUM

...................I can perceive your bared sternum in the V..........................

....the perfumed............................

....

....planar

.........bone with the..

............jasmine hint.........has to be touched softly as I see the hardest...........................

....body parts as vulnerable.........................

....

....and the raw edged V is.............

.....splitting downward towards the reverse V of the crotch..................................

....as you.....................................

...............perhaps...

...........................want to be torn in half...

...............rather than endure...the hurt.................

....of desire...........................

....

....or you want your plunging

necklines to display...

....how expectations...........................

....can split to reveal a warrior's breastplate...

....

....you cannot be afraid......to grab both sides..............

.....of the V....and rip them further to bare..........the revered sternum...........................

....prized....

....and viewed in the rough frame...................

......although it is a simulated vulnerability..

....at least simulated vulnerability is bearable....

....for those...

.................................who cannot...

withstand unreasonable tenderness...

....

.............and I love the open V-necks of people in photographs......as they are unashamed...

....to be so beautiful...

.............with their bravery exemplified in the sternum.............as I want to press my hand

...................against it to reassure...

.........................myself of the bone strength...

....I value open-necked shirts or tunics.....

........because they launch the bare skin..

........................and release the excruciating warmth from the chest...........................

....

....although you want to tear...............................

....the V down a further frontal seam............so that you.......

....can molt or reform yourself.........................

....

...........or just pull at yourself with an ecstasy like a heat...

....you want the tanned or untanned neck.....

.......adorned only..............with the carotid artery..

....

....because you admire..................

.................the drama of minimal exposure...

.........as though..

...............................the V was formed..

...........by an expansion...........of demureness..

....

....

....I prefer the unfinished edges of the V because.........the.....

..............frayed borders seem infinite...

.....................and I cannot bear to refine the torn V..............or alter...........................

.....................the presentation of the exposed sternum...

....as one can only wear the unsewn moral.................

.......or immoral open-necked shirt with a beautiful result...

....

....and the deflection of the bony sternum....

.............like a display of a..........surface from.....which..

....all the necklaces are torn off at last...

....

..........the naturally shining sternums..

...............................you want to wear..

...............a slit-front rough-hewn V..

................because you desire the unconcealment..

...............................revealed by the flaring lapels..

....

....and you have the desire to widen the tear.....................

....

.....................................and to deform your collars as you cannot exist.....................

........in common shirts anymore..

.............and want...........the cut neck.......of a beaver-lined sack yanked over your head...

...............................and the bared void........of the..

.............neckline sharpened...

.........to a downward.......point.........with the edges rolled back as you breathe...............

....beneath it...

....you want to be released from plain shirts at once

and shown to the world...

....

....with all the gold medallions removed...................

....so that the value remains with the body........................

....

.......as you have wanted..

..............to trust your imperfections...

..................................and.............deepen the neck...

..............as you.....have many bare surfaces to unveil...

....

.............................and yet conceal yourself.....in order to flaunt a reverse feeling..........

.....which is pride...

....

SUNBURNS

...............aha........the forgotten sunburns of my girlhood!.....................................

....when I could not be touched...............

....

.......................when I had to lie...on clean sheets alone...

......and try to think...of what I had done wrong..............

....

.......................I remember when I was dangerously sunburned and I was glowing.............

....and everyone tried to................

....smear creams...............................

...........................on my shoulder blades..

...............and I had to lie....................................gingerly and gingerly.................

....

....on clean hotel sheets..

....

...........and gleam...............with clear aloe gel...

....

...................as everyone else went to dinner..

....

....when I had.

...........................burned eyelids...a burned nape.....

......of my neck..

....

.........................an entire...................outline of a swimsuit.....burned.......................

....

....and yet............

........the satisfaction of it...

....

...................the physical shininess..

....

....as a child..........

....I was...............................

...............red hot and very lonely..........

THE TORTURERS

When I was a young girl, my parents hated me and wouldn't give me the right kind of food. I used to steal Barbies and hide them in unique places all over the house, but I took no joy in it. One Sunday, my parents discovered the Bridal Barbie I had hidden in the freezer when one of her shoes fell out of the ice dispenser into my father's drink. Immediately, they put me into the car and drove me away from the house, throwing the Bridal Barbie out of the window of the car so that she bounced on the road and lost her veil.

They left me at a pawn shop with a carousel horse in the window. The pawn shop owner took care of me for many years and let me play with the antique spurs. I became an expert in pricing the boxes of cutlery brought in by disenchanted chefs from the nearby culinary school and presided over the display cases of penknives and nacre switchblades which I sold to delinquents. Often I would write tiny notes and tape them to the blades so that when the people got home and pushed the button they would see a message like, "The powerful force of this knife is now unleashed."

One time a vagrant came into the pawn shop and tried to pawn a harmonica. He said, "The music comes out of it like a knife." It took me a while to become proficient with the precious harmonica. I used to warm it under my arms as I slept by the various blue dumpsters on my way across the land with the vagrants. As my skill with the harmonica increased, the listening vagrants insisted that I play for them. So, every night I played and was not ever beaten or punched. At that time I wanted to swallow the harmonica, so vital was it to me. I became concerned with covering it with my hands so that none of the silver glinted. One night I let the harmonica slip from my mouth at the end of the song like a jaw falling off a rotting pharaoh. I played until I hated it and that was music.

Next I found a job in a restaurant which sold daiquiris. My job was to slice the lemons and limes that garnished the bright daiquiris in balloon glasses. I had developed many callouses on my hands from playing the harmonica and so the lemons and limes did not sting. I grew to admire the limes and lemons. They were more beautiful to me than the burgundy car my boss the millionaire drove. One day this lonely millionaire came into the restaurant and demanded that I let him cut the lemons. That night I had a vision. Then I forgot about the vision. Later, I quit that job.

For a long time after this, I did not take any pleasure in life. As I could not find another job I liked and would not go back to the dumpsters, I used to stand on the docks. When a man invited me onto a boat, I agreed, but did not take much pleasure in the man although he was excellent at pulling up shiny tuna which gave me somber memories about my harmonica. My only interest during this time was to sit on the prow of the boat. I would often do this for about 5–6 hours. One morning I woke up from sleeping with the man who was not even snoring, looked in the mirror and suddenly punched myself in the eye.

After that, the man let me off on the dock so I could walk the highways. I walked the highways for years and passed several billboards until I came to a ballroom surrounded by dust swirls. This was the torturer's ballroom. I got a job as a mirror washer in the ballroom and washed all the mirrors with blue chemicals. As I spent my time looking in mirrors, I began to realize that I had never seen the torturers who danced and screamed at night. One night I ran down the halls into the small room that was the coat-check room where I buried my face in the torturers' coats. When the coat-check girl returned for the coats, I hid myself in a long ermine cloak. So when the head torturer put me on I wrapped my arms around her like an ermine maiden. And that is how I became head torturer.

CHAMPAGNE

.................you are alone with..

....

...........unstable champagne on your teeth..

....and you swallow flecks..........of it..............

....

....

....and then it keeps rumbling in your glass............................

....the wet..............

................lukewarm fluid in your oral cavity..

....

....

....granular...

....

.................controllable champagne..

....poured downward...................................

....

....

....as you lick the corpuscles...................

..........or spores of burst carbonation...

....

....

....and rub................

your nose with the sleeve...of your fuzzy.........................

....sweater....................

....and push all the chairs...

....................out of your way...

....

........................and crush...

....thistles and thistles of soft foam........with the fulcrum........

....

....of your jaw...

..........and swallow the ruptured....drink...

....

......as a translucent inset of your larnyx...

..........reveals...

....

....

..........rivulets........in your throat...

....and you reach the doorframe...................

....

..........chewing the droplets..

....................like the ephemeral gristle of triumph!..

...........as champagne trickles down your neck...

......as you are smiling...

....

....................the level ascends and ascends in more champagne glasses.........................

....

....

....as you are....................................

....straining your cardigan...........sweater........

....

....with the heels of your pumps stuck to the balcony........

..........................popping pearl sweater buttons.... . . .

FLASH

you have to walk towards your goal...

....

....which is the opening split of a flashbulb.........

..........which feels.........like sunlight shucked from an oyster shell...................................

....

......and be..struck with the...

.................flashes that have milky fuses..

....and bask...

..............in the glare of..........silver lockets...........banged open on sea rocks...............

..........as the centres.......................sizzle and deform..

.................and you replace...

......................................the faceted metal flash-shields...

....

.............................and the shimmering hammered...

....light inflates....................

........and falls upon you like a net..

....

....and the blackened cases....................................

...................crash to the floor..

60

.......after the clench of a slender fuse...........................a plume of smoke unfurls.............

.................and all the birds..

....

....fly out of the tall grass........................

....

.......you have to face the tumescent bulbs...

................as you walk through a doorway of shark jaws...

....

.........................and flashes..

....hollow out the bases...........................

...........of other flashes...

....and a thistle of light skates along an edge.............

and..

...................the light........squeezes and squeezes itself brighter.................................

....in a vise......................

.....as..the larvae of a vision matures.........................

................and bursts the glass.......and blows..

a visual glaze...

...............before..

......................you hear..
.........the croak of the flash..
....and you frown in your beautiful portrait

ELECTRONIQUE

I'm afraid my madness will manifest as paradise...

....

..................................and that I will have to be strapped down............................

.............because of my happiness...

....which is like.........

...icicles...........................or an electronic spider lily.......................................

....

....and I'm afraid my reality will melt..........

...................to form the liquid alloy.....of reality...

......which is...........a neural flower pavilion...

....

....with..

....free-rolling Ferris wheels...

....

.........................and an irreversible..

.............pressure of temperamental......sweetness in the pineal gland...........which...........

....is like......................

.............a pearl-handled vise.....................turned until.....................................

.it...

....ruptures...

...........to reopen the unreal palisade....................or planetarium of lunacy.................

.......................or hanging garden....of sadness...

.............................where there are...

.........phosphorescent blue....butterflies...............and...

....black-eyed goldfish.............................

....

...........and a generated atmosphere...

.........that has......a vibrating.........botanical.............pheromone............................

..............or chypre scent...

.....................with recorded.........turtledoves...

....

..............or overlapping.....watersprings............................with the expanding.......

......hologram of watermists...

....

....as....................

.............an alpha wave of euphoria...

.....................or a moment like a...

...........................slit in an unseen bandwidth...

..........................or a flexed-open.....unknown seam bears..................................

....an epicentre.....................................

....like a persimmon.........

....

..........as lovebirds.....unlock and cascade...

....out of the branches....................

.............and flow and compress between the tree trunks.................................

....

....swiveling in a flexible unison..............................

....

..through computer-generated cloud formations..with pink/orange clouds..and lightning bolts.

...................and pterodactyls......in the daylight.....................................

....

....my madness remodeled..............................

............on the plain muse of a white phalaenopsis.......................................

....

....as I am surrounded................................

...................by phototropic organisms of insanity.......................................

...............................or filmy man-o'-wars...

....and internal topiary............projected externally.........

....

.................and electronically plotted..............clusters of tsetse flies.........................

....

...............I exist in a blister of fantasy...

.................and ripen with a dire....optimism...

....................................as the continuum of space-time........bulges...........................

...........to bear a deformed sphere...

......................filled with the gloss of my madness..

.....................................which is the illusion..

.........................of the lava flow or the supperating bliss...

...............of rainbows in a brain scan...

.............or the implosion of a stained glass dome...

....

.............or the formation...

.........................in my mind...

.....................................of an atrocious....happiness..

......and mental gaudiness..

....and a permanent state..

...................of arousal in the blood cells............sired...

by the dagger plunge of the fire-orange genital of the bird of paradise.....

THE AQUAMARINE

The aquamarine becomes invisible when you place it into the sea. It seems like birds should have aquamarine beaks that they can dip into the sea and therefore surprise the fish. They could also sing aquamarine songs. If you borrowed someone's aquamarine, swallowed it, and jumped into the sea, then you would not become invisible. But your soul would become visible and all the fish would try to bite you. If you put an aquamarine onto any surface other than the sea, then it should be visible. If you put on an aquamarine choker and look in the mirror and don't see anything, then you must be the sea.

FENCE was launched in the spring of 1998. A biannual journal of poetry, fiction, art and criticism, **FENCE** has a mission to publish challenging writing and art distinguished by idiosyncrasy and intelligence rather than by allegiance with camps, schools, or cliques. **FENCE** has published works by some of the most esteemed contemporary writers as well as excellent work by complete unknowns. It is part of our mission to support young writers who might otherwise have difficulty being recognized because their work doesn't "fit in" to either the mainstream or to accepted modes of experimentation.

FENCEbooks is an extension of that mission; with our books we hope to provide expanded exposure to poets and writers whose work is excellent, challenging, and truly original. The Alberta Prize is an annual series launched in 2000 by **FENCEbooks** in conjunction with the Alberta duPont Bonsal Foundation. The Alberta Prize offers publication of a first or second book of poems by a woman, as well as a $5,000 cash prize underwritten by the Alberta duPont Bonsal Foundation.

The Alberta duPont Bonsal Foundation was started in 2000 as a living memorial to Alberta duPont Bonsal, a woman of exceptional vitality, love and compassion. Her mother, Josephine Brinton duPont Grimm, an artist and writer, developed in her a lifelong interest in the arts. The Foundation's mission is to "expand and enrich the circles of inspiration that are Josephine's and Alberta's legacies, allowing those legacies to benefit the larger communities of region, nation and world." Each year, the Foundation will honor outstanding women poets and visual artists who have not yet attained national recognition. Honorees will receive opportunities for exhibition, publication and purchase of their work. The Foundation's goal is "to further the artist's career and productivity at the time in her artistic development when such aid can be put to greatest use."

FENCEbooks' second prize series is the **Fence Modern Poets Series**, published in cooperation with **saturnalia books**. This contest is open to poets of either gender and at any stage in their career, be it a first book or fifth.

For more information about either prize, visit our website at www.fencebooks.com, or send an SASE to **FENCEbooks** /[Name of Prize], 14 Fifth Avenue, #1A, New York, NY 10011.

To see more about **FENCE** visit www.fencemag.com.